First of Pisces

First of Pisces

Poems by

James Scannell McCormick

Cover design by Shay Culligan

ISBN: 978-1-952326-24-0

Kelsay Books
502 South 1040 East, A-119
American Fork, Utah, 84003

for Elizabeth Sachs

Acknowledgments

Grateful acknowledgment is made to these publications, in which the following poems first appeared:

"Consequences": *Plainsongs*

"Copernicus and Rheticus at Frombork": *THINK* 6.2

"Eight-Tapers Charm": Maria W. Faust Sonnet Contest, 2016

"Four Orthodox Jews Swimming at Nice": *Rotary Dial*

"Intermezzo for Charlie": *Verse Wisconsin*

"Photograph of Isabella Blow, In a Hat": *Better Than Starbucks!*

"Sundogs Above Stockholm (*Vädersolstavlan*)": *Penwood Review*

"Rikard Lane": Maria W. Faust Sonnet Contest, 2015

"Scene from the Life of St. Godelieve," "St. Savior in Chora, Istanbul": *Dappled Things*, Fall 2013

"Writing Washington Island": *Fifth Washington Island Literary Festival*

The poems in *Four Quarters* first appeared in *The Elements,* © Finishing Line Press, 2020.

Contents

Vergings

Canon of the Science of Triangles

Four Quarters

1. First of Pisces

In spring when woods are getting green
I'll try and tell you what I mean.
      —Carroll

Sun sets still blue but later, by skyline's cold minutes,
To the sun-spun world's tilt from true, until day
And night, like green sunfish slit gills to tailfin, split

And match: even, now, at last. You used to say
It's September that you like best—fat cattails, elms' rough
Yellows. Not this slop and bluster: Crust of gray snow

And tussock. Stunned boxelder bugs that might flick to life.
Or not. You used to wince, mock the prairie's mad
Bordering, the bleakness of its flat ache—but as if

That ache were a fault. *Because* a fault, a need—
Not forgiven. Not by half. As if you were afraid
Of that wary edge, thick as breath, thin as blood.

2. Kalamazoo Sunset

Drenched scent of Lake Michigan's wary west edge pressed lintels,
Jambs the day you were born, above slaggy shore lip-
Thin, lip-tight. Here, west wind carries that scent still,

Though miles inland: fog-green water's heavy lift and dip.
But your first look from the east beaches: bluffs' slow
Break, slow slide; then across sand's bright, horizon-wide slope;

Waves' tang—even here, where solid, stolid Dutch once grew
Celery and the Word, and shiftless sunset dawdles over roof-
Line of a dead mall, its blistered lot of rows

Of wan lines. You'll watch as fireflies strike and snuff
Their yellow-green flames. You'll want to say that here's enough
For you, enough for you to take, from one life.

3. Writing Washington Island

From one life—surge and churn as the ferry yaws,
Sidles Plum Island's sharp brink of shoals and white pine,
Thrums into harbor—*into another*. A threshold: water, earth. You

Step—not, naturally, your first. But even so you begin,
You verge. And aren't words a verge, a crossing over,
A crossing above, like a ferry's: above sunk ships' bones—

Drift-pin, keelson, capstan—where the shallow channel's quiet
     water
Hovers cold. Even day and night halve. To passing sun
Hidden raspberries grow sweet and soft, and beaches bleach their

Stones, big as loaves. Night hefts its moonless balance-pans
Of new-cut stars. So come. Become. In this one
Life, after any other. You're already apart. You've already begun.

4. Bleak Midwinter Blues

And so you begin: A blue ring around the moon.
Orion's belt, its three stars thinning blue-black to night.
Elm and last fall's lawn flattening black to shadow between

Sky's blue plates. An hour, with leaving behind, and out—
Snow-blue skin under the eye, under the wrist. Lost
Blue of tattoos on the shin, of tear-blue cigarette

Smoke. In a room Christmas boughs let drop their first
Blue needles, one by one. Something familiar, then forgotten—
        two
Dead pens. Blue-lined paper. A love poem. And last,

You at a quiet window of drifts, of a raw
Day's blue bones of ice. Your cold hands, empty now
To early sunset. To an hour. To another. Cold. Blue.

Piano Pieces for Dogs

Intermezzo for Charlie

It's all in the left hand, says your mistress. *Brahms*
Is all in the left hand. Why does she bother
With the piano at all, Charlie, you stretching from flews

To dewclaws on the sleepy carpet, and your leash hanging
So unoccupied behind the door? Hot August afternoons and scent
Of the salt sea—those are the days that should

Be yours, dog: your pushed-in muzzle was bred for
No good reason except to gnaw your rump and stub
Of tail, to snap at the frenzied buzz of rainbow

Scarabs. Shaking the phlegm from your eyes, you're the guardian
Of Belmont Heights, of the quiet limit of the world.
Hey, Boo! Hey, Booger! Hey, Monkey-face, Pig-face! calls

Your master, who makes skinned tennis balls drop miraculously
    from
The absolute blue of heaven. Why shouldn't the whole world
Be Monterey jack in your dish, chew toys and scairdy-

Cats, Thai-beef morsels, watchbands, and ice-cubes that you
Take so delicately in your underbiting jaws? You live in
A truer grace: *Good boy! Yeah! What a good boy!*

Ballade for Archie

(St. Patrick's Day)

They mean no good, Archie, those careening, green-clad revelers,
And you know it: rigid on a Turkish *kilim* whose
Weft your rump has rubbed thin, you press your blunt

Snout—going white—to the window and wallop with barking
The midmorning air. Boozy, hatted and beaded, duos or trios
Are overspreading Allentown, are ever lurching from the curb to

Try to sneak a wobbly piss on the crisp daffodils
Along the side property line that you yourself watchfully mark.
Only when you know that your sobering warning has cleared

The beery sidewalk will you coil beneath the rebuilt Baldwin,
Just an hour earlier filled with tilting sunlight and Chopin,
To hold in your half closed eyes' brown corner that

Hateful electric fan, and scent the air for toast; or
You'll shake your undocked ears, flop at the stair top,
And doze to far-off caterwauling of "Danny Boy," twitch

As you dream, maybe of St. Patrick himself, tugging off
His shamrock embroidered gloves and laying down his golden
      crosier
To squat and scratch the brindling of your rapturous flanks.

Impromptu for Cooper

So your lead wrenches, steel teeth of your collar bite—
Your great heart, Cooper, makes you headstrong. Your litter's runt,
You now buck and plunge, lunge and jump and floor

Everyone because, really, who hasn't been bowled over by love?
Be good! Be good, or put you out! Caged, disgraced,
You—puzzled, buffaloed—blink as though to protest that if

You aren't good, then what can good be? The length
Of a Schubert tune brings reproach and release—and you're
At it again, neither sadder nor wiser: you'll still mewl

And grunt outside every door closed to you. A lifted
Index finger, and you squat on your fawn-red hocks,
Hope for a drop of yolk, a dollop of butter.

Let those Kronenbourg roses go blowzy, drop their spent, inedible
Petals; let that fence halt your advance to the parlor.
And let all the scandalized, slandering neighbor folk hound you:

In the yard sits your favorite red ball, adrift in
Lake Erie's gift of April snow. You'll bray, yawp, yip
And bawl, giving tongue and full throat to your joy.

Sequence:
In Memoriam S.S.M

Poem that Repeats a Line from Bishop

September rain falls on the house. Too late
To save lawn now scorched to thatch. Blowsy
Geraniums, marigolds wallow in swilled pots
As chilled wasps drown in an algae-fuzzy

Birdbath. Heavy-wet sky sags cold gray just
Beyond reach; a little metal sundial stands
Mute on its rusted tripod. Powdery must
Has killed the cinnamon zinnias. Roses bend

With weight of rotting hips. *September rain*
Falls on the house. Gutters, splash-blocks overflow,
Splatter quoins, corbel, drown torpid Asian
Lady beetles. From cold rooms unlit windows

Look out on a snarled trumpeter vine that lowers
Its rangy red tendrils and will never flower.

First Snow in Mellon Park

Pittsburgh

Yesterday, sun buffed the Ohio, the Craftsman
Row houses in Squirrel Hill, Shadyside. Today,
Snow sifts through maple leaves thin
And cold as gold. In Mellon Park, gray

Granite steps still rise with the hill, wait
Decorously. No need: The threshold's chilled.
The 40s took the mansion. Then, soot
Would settle like snow. Now, below blasted

Mascarons, where Doucet's draperies once trailed,
Dogs piss. Brick-red alleys still stumble on
To where, along a bowed, chipping balustrade,
Ferns and thin centifolias, damasks weaken.

Persephone, gone to black lichen and coal-smoke,
Holds her marble pomegranate to dark and flakes.

Shrouded House

Isn't this a kind of house for the dead,
The dead who should be mindful, but never are?
All Saints', All Souls', Guy Fawkes's plot of botched
Gunpowder—while slow dust-motes settle, powder

Stiffened Wal-Mart poly-cotton bed-sheets
Over armchair, bookcase, bed, and fire-screen.
Shelves and fridge are empty-bellied, the heat's
Turned down. The stairway's dim and still, even

The ceiling fans wrapped. In the mirror's breathless
Frame uncertain ghosts could appear, could start
And chill: among these palls their own weightless
Image, lost and caught. Forgotten. But they don't.

It's just a house with doors and windows sealed,
With rooms where no one's ever really lived.

Post-Christmas Carol

Snow from a third or fourth fall: unwelcome,
Banked up heavy and tired. Then thaw. Or rain
That freezes, seals tindery cedar trim
Around lintels, and stubby bulbs of lines

Of Christmas lights, their edgeless, unearthly blue
The disbanded heavenly host's faux afterglow.
Daylight's a holidays-only churchgoer who
Slips in late and sneaks out early. A row

Of brittle, tinsel stripped tannenbaums leans
Into an unplowed street. In garages split
Boxes and packages stuff recycling bins;
Ash of tissue and ribbon lies in grates.

In kitchens bought carnations' petals brown,
While rinds of uneaten Spanish clementines harden.

Eight Tapers Charm

No lewd fish, no fruit, no wide-eyed bird
About to fly its cage...

       —Mahon

The first for doors—threshold, doorpost, lintel,
Hinge, and lock, for beginnings, endings, for word
To be said, for word now said, now dead; for fall
Of weak sunlight, for womb, for tomb, for void

Of mouthless, monthless winter, for time's whiteout.
The second for starving red-tailed hawks that line
Miles of highway. The third for suicide white
Of the Cold Moon. The fourth and the fifth for bone-

Chilling, for breath-killing cold, for candleblack
Sky, for sleep, for sleep of ice, of ground-freeze.
The sixth for Fish-Goat, the seventh for single oak,
For whitefish held in thick water and ooze.

The eighth for the black, implacable gods of lack,
Of ordeal, of thwarting, of looking ahead, and back.

Rikard Lane

Natchitoches

In the ditch roadside, ibises raise to daylight
And spent tulips the sharp arc of their wings'
White. In the garden fire-ants pick vermiculite
Between rosemary and scrubby mint dozing

Through midmorning. Around noon a collarless
Fice arrives to nose through daffodil stalks
Taller than she is. Past crimson Japanese
Camellias, sunlight leans against the back

Fence with fidgety, finger-thin lizards.
Towards sunset turtledoves call in the redbuds;
From the crape myrtle the cats slip from the yard.
Then moonrise: beneath unopened magnolia buds

Raccoons root, then trundle off; in the field
A shadowy mare dreams a gift of Jonagolds.

Four Orthodox Jews Swimming at Nice

Who so cocky to chance the grim sea that's been
Grinding forever the Côte d'Azur (now gray,
Like sea, like horizon) into loaves of stone?
Teenaged boys. Below the preoccupied *Quai*—

Joggers, mostly, and a clutch of shivery sightseers—
They've defied riptide and hanging rain to lunge,
Naked and whole, into the sullen breakers.
After they towel goose-fleshed thighs and ribcage,

They dress: tallit katan over shoulders
Itchy with salt, kippa pinned and clinging
To sandy scalp. As the others don their trousers,
The nearest skips stones, his tzitzyot swinging.

Tomorrow, the lavender-scented Mistral will blow,
Bending beachwards the palms at L'Hôtel Negresco.

Sundogs Above Stockholm *(Vädersolstavlan)*

20 April 1535

First, the night-watch, passing the southern gate,
Saw; then creeping street-sweepers, who leaned on worn
Besoms and squinted up; then even flushed
Bakers abandoned ovens fired at dawn

And gazed: in air grainy with ice crystals,
The sun six-fold, the sky above *Storkyrkan*'s
Steeple swiped with chords and rainbow-edged circles
Through mare's-tail gray of cirrus clouds. Omens—

But from whom? God or devil? And of what? Divine
Displeasure at sacked abbeys, bishops with wives?
Infernal lure for the godly to turn them again
Into the triple-tiara'd Whore's bond-slaves?

At nine the parhelia bleached to unclear heaven,
And Masses—in Swedish, by royal decree—began.

Photograph of Isabella Blow, in a Hat

[T]o keep everyone away from me. They say, Oh, can I kiss you? I say, No,
thank you very much. That's why I've worn the hat. Goodbye. I don't want to
be kissed by all and sundry. I want to be kissed by the people I love.
                    —Isabella Blow, when asked why she always wore a hat.

Jolie laide, she holds the world the distance
Of redoubled velvet brim and featherbone. Smoke
From her Benson and Hedges strokes the camp elegance
Of a tight boa, maribou afterfeathers black,

Softly crosshatched. Her brother, two, had drowned
In rainwater. Shaking hands, her mother had gone
For good. At Hilles the pewter cutlery is crowned
With ivory heads (knives the Duke of Wellington,

Bonaparte the forks), a flock of Soay shits
Where they please, but *Haud muto factum* her family's
Motto: *I have a plan,* she'll say. *But I'm not*
Telling you. She'll try a jump from an overpass.

Pills and vodka. Finally, a tin of Paraquat.
Rising black from her coffin's roses, a hat.

in memoriam
d. 7 May 2007

35

St. Savior in Chora

Istanbul

For six centuries the Emperor's double walls
Have cinched the seven hills of New Rome, though
Cats now prowl the peribolus, and limestone falls
Into the seedy leeward *cadde* where two

Urchins beg for *kuruş*. Beyond the Gate
Of Charistos, through which the Conqueror passed, gather
The low domes of Kariye Camii, light
Inside floating clusters of Greek letters—

Themselves half inflammable seraph—above
Frescoes, unearthly in freshness: Peter and Paul,
Joseph, the Virgin in prayer, Adam and Eve.
In an arch, Metochites, onion-turbaned, kneels,

Offers Christ Pantocrator, indigo-swathed,
The church itself, light as a loaf of bread.

(Sonnet for a) Blue Devil

after Cruikshank

Encore te membrera des moz.
—Ordo Repraesentationis Adae

Noon, but you don't fret about your shadow:
The Lord's Day sky is wan and damp. Naturally,
I'm late—born that way (four days). At the window
Table, you tap your goat's-foot. Unnaturally

Red, your goatee burns, a single flame.
A look of no surprise (*What were you
Expecting? Horns? A pitchfork?),* you're the same:
Listening like a confessor. But this time through,

I sin. I omit jeering imps, and black-
Clad beadle, and—head-strapped, mallet in fist—
Coffin-maker, his burden on his back:
All your boys. Then, over eggs, you list

Your favorite snares—the tongue, the pen—for me:
I feel a chill where my soul used to be.

Vienna, Again

This was then. A train-car rattling its tracks
Through stolid Alps. A loaf, chunks of Muenster:
We were poor, the hostel full. Forced to wander
Like Habsburg ghosts, we faded along with wicks

Flickering a dawn Mass at the Dom. It took
Our last *Schilling* to pay to stand through *Tannhäuser,*
Then share a slice of dense torte at the Sacher.
And this is now. Strangers' flat in a freak

Heat-wave—sleep a sweaty drowse. My German
Thirty years in wasting. Schönbrunn's *Gloriette*
Still patrolled by dowdy sphinxes. The long-

Suffering, shackled Danube. At Belvedere, throngs
Of parasoled Spaniards. The Dom, ungainly, daylit.
Café Hawelka: a demitasse, drunk alone.

Vergings

Blijde Inkomst

Joan the Mad at Antwerp, August 1496

*Her future husband's failure to welcome [Joan] when she stepped ashore at
Middelburg also presaged enduring problems. [....] Upon reaching Antwerp,
[Joan] suffered from fever and took to bed for several days.*

—Aram

At nine years old she'd cried when she learned that she couldn't
    wear her skeleton, radius
And pearled ulna balanced on damask whorls of her sleeves belling
    heavily to cuffs

Of back-turned black velvet. *"Mas, Alteza..."* Miranda, her
    maestro, had blinked, held his
Smooth palms inward and before the black cloak at his ribcage,
    had gestured quickly, twice, as

If beckoning. But she wouldn't be comforted. Sixteen now, fever
    rocks her in its slow hull
Like, at Portsmouth, her becalmed Genoese carrack. But then, as it
    lurched off Zeeland—a gull

Shrills, yanks her up and out into a burgher's great draped bed
    hung with sick odor
Of bleach and sea air. One woman—no, two—murmuring in
    Dutch, soft *tink* of pewter

Ewer against pewter basin, then shadow, quick, quick as that
    glance she used to catch—
That she used to believe she'd caught—in her mother's shrewd,
    shaded face: cross-hatch

Of bewilderment and insistence. Fever is the wharf empty at
    Middelburg, is the sea's heave
Now in the quay stones: nowhere the bridegroom. Politic
    apologies to the mutter and shove [...]

Of the crowd, and on a single ribbon, a single pendant ruby had
       jittered and sung with her
Jugulars: fever the slight incline of her head, fever scalp's prickle
       under her hood. Fever

Is the thinnest Aragonese edge in her French, is the vortex of gulls
       above the Antwerp quay,
Is pursuit, is pursuit. Now she lies, salt-sick as the sunken carrack,
       as her soaked trousseau,

Damask sleeves now belling to the sea-floor's black. To drowned
       deckhands, their sea-
Cold fingers black and curled beside the curled, stirring pages of
       her bloated breviary.

Laten we het raam een beetje openen. A window, panes round and
       thick as wine
Bottles' punts, swings open, then a lightest outdrawing of bleach-
       draped air – no more than

Just stirs and pulls the stiff and figured bed-hangings, ruby-black,
       just stirs the room where
She lies alone: no more than a breath, no more than one breath, in
       fever, pursues another.

La Remise: Marie Antoinette at the Île des Épis

April 1770

She is naked. In silence even her snuffling pug has been taken.
    Then fingers on
Her forearms, moving them away from her hips. Stockings from
    Lyon,

From Paris a silk chemise shimmery-cool as water: she is being
    made
Into the Dauphine. Thrum of rain. She can make out, in the
    borrowed

Tapestry darkening with wet, a gold-eyed princess who watches as
    a gold-
Haired prince reaches for…She can't say. Outside, at the head of
    the stilled

Cavalcade, her *berline* had rocked to rest, its rear wheels on soaked
Hapsburg soil, its front wheels on a rain-shiny bridge as the pocked

Rhine eased past the island. Outside, sodden green of high spring.
    Soft-
Tipped pines and chain-trees drip. In the slow shallows white
    storks lift,

Lower their bills to stir for frogs. Inside, no one speaks. Drafts,
    damp. Odor
Of molding wood, of rain, of the great river. Her palms' heels
    brush the panniers

Beneath cloth-of-gold. On her back something is being pulled,
    tied. Thunder
Above the Schwarzwald, then metal-on-leather jingling of
    frightened horses' gear—[…]

Reins, stirrup. She had been sleeping in the apartments of her
      mother the Empress,
All rooms hung in black velvet of mourning: her father, the
      Emperor. As

Tapers shivered, she had dreamed of the red frockcoats of
      Laxenburg, of sledges by
Torchlight, had awakened to believe herself there, in her bedroom
      with high

Painted sweet-peas climbing to a ceiling of larks. Her neckline is
      adjusted, and she
Is done. Behind her in the dimness her retinue stands, hands
      finally quiet. The unsteady,

Subtle thrum that she now hears is blood in her own jugulars. As
      of itself the door
To the dank, chill *salle* opens to take her—flush-throated, alone—
      into a remade forever.

Consequences

Lewis Carrol's Last Photograph of Alice, Oxford, 1870

It's too late to correct it, said the Red Queen: *when you've once said a thing,
that fixes it, and you must take the consequences.*
                                        —Through the Looking-Glass

Neither he nor she says a thing. She's sitting, posed. And he's
        telling
The seconds that make light and silver nitrate into something not
        painting,

Not sight. Into a kind of world. Into a kind of double of *this*
        world, only
Where color becomes lost, where her pale lavender day-dress will
        become gray,

Darker gray her exactly flattened *aubergine* hair-bow, as though in
        a pencil
Sketch. But that can never be colored in. She sits so still that she
        can feel,

Laced tight in its ribcage, her heart, also telling: telling the times
        that she's
Done this before. That *he's* done this before—made her into a
        Chinese

Girl in shivery silks, a beggar-child, a May-queen with a hawthorn
        crown,
The leaves in the print shining black: a kind of world. Eighteen

Since May, she wonders if, for this photograph, she's herself: not
        even
Props—no fern spindly in its pot, no lapful of black cherries. No
        straw sun- […]

45

Hat to slant beneath her curved fingers as she lay pretending to
      sleep:
He'd told her to. Just as she'd told him to tell a story during the
      rowing-trip

To Godstow. He told it, Holsteins and bored hayricks heavy
      against the river.
Was she *that* girl then—the girl falling slowly into a low hall of
      locked doors?

Or the girl in the slim boat, the girl sitting still as he made a world
      around
Her, or a *kind* of her, of this world? Neither she nor he says a
      thing, but behind

Her head, cracks pock and chip and split the wall. And forever
      will: The wall
Could be remade, could be replastered, repainted olive or Prussian
      blue or teal—

No matter, in that double, not painting, not sight. She, too: she'll
      be forever posed,
Forever uncolored. Unspeaking. Waiting for him to tell her into a
      world. Fixed.

Darkening Room

Clover Adams Drinks Potassium Cyanide, Washington, D.C., 1885

How true it is that the mind sees what it has means of seeing.
                        —in a letter to her father

Light has become for her a leaving, a lack. She'll think, *One says,*
"Light leaves the sky," as it does now, through chilled midday
        haze,

Through junipers and immature sycamores, gawky and splayed, in
Lafayette Park. She'll think, *One says, "Light retreats,"* like
        McClellan

Before Lee from jittery Richmond, like winter withdrawing to
        solstice,
Standstill of the sun as though pressed to gel and paper between
        glass

Plates. Withdrawing like, at her shut summer house, unquiet
Tide of the sickening Atlantic pulling back from the cloud-lit

Strand below Smith's Point: empty. Lack is light sliding from her
Desktop, empty of the Sunday letters she would write to her father.

April, a bright blur of redbuds, pulled him away, who had stood
        straight
As a shaft of light. At his ending, he could no longer swallow.
        And yet

She'd try to pull back to herself: June, at the azalea-red edge of
The Alleghenies' backwards slide, or October, in a carriage,
        hooves'

Dusty thud to the District's receding streets, she'd speak as she'd
        once been able [...]

To, then suddenly stop, press her forehead, as if to call back the
      chemical
Spells of her first times photographing: *pyrogallic acid six grains*
To two ounces water…ammonia one ounce…alum saturate
      solution—

Ten minutes for the negative. For flat absence. She'll think, *I'm*
      not real—
No more than what's captured through an aperture in a mahogany
      box. She'll

Leave behind a fading day, a darkening room—sun gray, shadow
      white;
Leave behind ghost-scent of bitter almonds, and a vial of empty
      light.

Timing

Mary ("Mae") O'Donnell Keane, Last of the "Radium Girls," *at the Waterbury Clock Factory, Connecticut, 1924*

Can you tell me, Mary O'Donnell, how long eternity is? asked
      Monsignor.
His biretta's weft deflected shifted light. She was seven then, with
      her

Second-grade class, who sat in two rows days before First
      Communion.
Monsignor had come to examine them. But she couldn't answer.
      No one

Could. A single *tunk*: the wall clock shouldered its minute hand to
      eight,
The numeral that her brush's camelhair now dabs. The curves—
      tight,

Slightly raised—catch, spread the bristles. Still, she won't lip-
      point, sharpen
With her mouth the brush tipped with that bitter paint, gritty, palest
      yellow-green.

Instead she smooths her brush on the paint-saucer: rim to dial.
      Dial to rim.
*I'll tell you. Imagine the North Star made all of steel, and a
      sparrow, and him*

Flying from here to there. Ones and sevens are easiest: little
      flicks. But still
Not easy. Dial to rim. Rim to dial. Twelve numbers per dial, each
      dial

The size of a woman's palm. Eight cents per dial, twelve dials per
      tray—and of trays […]

No end. She finishes the eight. *Now, when the sparrow has flown all the long way*
To the North Star, he brushes just a wing against it, then turns back. She sits,
Now eighteen, one of twelve girls at high tables facing windows wide to July light

And—rarely, grudgingly—a puff of muggy air. She doesn't like this work:
Squint and finger-ache and back-cramp. Dial to rim. And she knows how quick

The other girls are; they count their work in trays. In missed serifs, she counts hers.
And however long it would take that sparrow's wing to wear away the North Star—

That *is eternity.* No clock in the studio—only handless dials. But from the windows—
She paints two down-strokes for an eleven—unnumbered flicks of wings: a sparrow.

in memoriam, 2014

Canon of the Science of Triangles

Georg Joachim de Porris, Known as Rheticus

*It is hard enough for us to work out what is on earth, wearisome to
know what lies within our reach; who, then,
can find out what is in the heavens?*

—Wisdom 9:16

1. Lindau

Winter 1547

Which of these three is the easiest to believe?
Bed-bound, breath-bound in sweat and superheated wave
Of fever dream, something had just started to heave

Him out of a lurching, spinning—out of nightmare:
His mother's soft call, a rising question, or prayer:
His own name. He'd been dreaming again of Meister

Copernik, who was holding him fast at the elbows,
Face so close that he could see the brows'
White streaks in the black; a lurching, spinning—"Giorgio."

"Giorgio, sleeping in the sun causes nightmares," gently says
His mother, a little sadly, a little urgently, lays
Back of her left hand just above his eyes,

To his left cheek. She turns towards the door,
Hushed slide of hem on floor straw; he hears,
From her right hand, a little clicking. Pearl tears:

A rosary. *First, the adjacent leg of a right*
Triangle: Our evil deeds will call forth evil spirits.
His mother has been begging, begging him to let

Her bring him to the Shrine of St. Eustace—
"To help you." But really she means, To exorcise
You. To unhouse from the freshly swept out house

Of his soul evil spirits who've moved back in.
No. No. This he doesn't believe. No go-between.
No heavenly pimp. Next to his headboard, Luther's own […]

Hymnal, lying open to two edge-worn quarto leaves:
"Aus tieffer not schrey ich zu dir": This saves.
He picks out the blunt tune from the staves.

2. Milan

Then for him it's June, after, but before: Sunrise
To prime at the cathedral, to measure of Ambrose's
Chant, to air clearer than any north, and skies

Close and clear as notes in a papist hymnal.
Every night for a week, outside the city walls,
He's lurked in bug-filled fields, gauged the epicycle

Of Venus whirling back from retrograde. *Second, the opposite*
Leg of the triangle: Love. In damp-soaked boots
He stands in the piazza, eyes closed to sun

Sweet and climbing—a lurching—"Maestro!"—his famulus,
        whose
Name is Giorgio, too. He scolds in naked Milanese:
Lugging is no chore for a scholar—lumbering pieces

Of triquetrum hoisted light as floor straw to left
Shoulder, to rest easy as a spear's ash shaft.
"For this work, you need the Bull," he laughs.

"Now, to bed!" So back to their room, squat
And grubby. Before he lets himself become helpless, lets
Himself be undressed and laid onto their ratty pallet,

He rifles his satchel and unpleats the natal chart—
Giorgio's. Nineteen last May. They sit, the younger alert
Yet boggled as he listens, the older doctorly, expert:

The sun in Taurus, but Taurus the rising sign,
So loyalty, courage, bodily strength—at this a grin
From Giorgio—a burningly passionate heart, but true one. […]

In Giorgio's low, drawn "Ah…!" awe and pleasure mingle.
"I'll show my fiancée!" And the sun sign's single
Square, at center, whirls the Houses. Each a triangle.

3. Frombork

Spring 1539

And third, the hypotenuse? Everything, everything is in motion!
In Meister Copernik's patient face, usually tranquil, a suggestion
Of humor, of passion. Of a long suffering admission:

Facts are absurd. Wild. Holy. Afloat in the canon's
Turricula, they pause, stand at an angle: the one,
Master, quadrant in his palm; the other, disciple, pen

Suspended, ready. Since vespers, damp daylight of late April
Has been leaking away, leaking down through roof tiles
Wind pried and slipping, above which gnat mad pipistrelles

Zigzag. Copernik has turned his head slightly, repeats in
A clean tone, "The sun doesn't move." The Empyrean
Is, of course, fixed. But everything else…"Even when—"

He adds, slyly, "you don't believe it." The slim
Flame by which he'd been writing jumps one time
As if suddenly troubled, undone, but then calms, comes

Back to a thin, stiff burn. Edge-sharp, he
Thinks, this *before* and *after*. His father, the stories
Went, housed a caged devil to torment for remedies

For his patients. In truth, his father tended them,
Cast their horoscopes. And stole. To spare the shame
Of hanging, he was beheaded. *Before:* his father's name.

After: None. He was thirteen then. Now, twenty-five,
He feels again a lurching, spinning…How to believe
The nauseating immeasurability of the universe? How to live […]

In it? Above, in the dimming sky, invisibly soar
White storks returning to the Vistula lagoon to pair.
Their wings' pure triangles cover and uncover the stars.

Notes

"First of Pisces": This phrase refers to the point at which the sun enters the constellation Pisces.

"Poem that Repeats a Line from Bishop": The line is taken from "Sestina."

"Eight Tapers Charm": The epigraphs is taken from Derek Mahon's "Courtyards in Delft."

"Sundogs Above Stockholm": The solar phenomenon depicted in the painting *Vädersolstavlan* occurred during the reign of Gustav I (Gustav Vasa), who established Lutheranism as the state religion of Sweden.

"Photograph of Isabella Blow, In a Hat": Fashion inspiration Isabella Blow committed suicide by drinking Parquat, a weed killer. This is the same manner in which her paternal grandfather had committed suicide as well.

"St. Savior in Chora": *"Cadde"* is Turkish for "street"; " *kuruş "* is a division of the *lira*, the Turkish currency.

"(Sonnet for a) Blue Devil": The title refers to a print by Cruikshank, the "blue devils," meaning "the blues" or sadness. The epigraph, taken from the Anglo-Norman *Jeu d'Adam,* is spoken by Satan to Adam and means, "You will remember those words."

"Blijde Inkomst": The title ("Joyeuse Entrée," in French) means the ceremony officially to receive into a city or country a member of the royalty. "Laten we het raam een beetje openen" is Dutch for "Let's open the window a bit."

About the author

James Scannell McCormick lives and teaches college English in Rochester, Minnesota. His first collection of poems, *The Song of Lies,* was published in April 2019 by David Robert Books; his second collection, *The Elements,* came out in March 2020 from Finishing Line Press.

www.ingramcontent.com/pod-product-compliance
Lightning Source LLC
Chambersburg PA
CBHW031153090426
42738CB00008B/1312